ZONE 13

The Shadow from the Past

DAVID ORME

Ransom

The Shadow from the Past
by David Orme
Illustrated by Jorge Mongiovi and Ulises Carpintero
Cover photograph: © jean-luc stadler

Published by Ransom Publishing Ltd.
Radley House, 8 St. Cross Road, Winchester, Hampshire, SO23 9HX, UK
www.ransom.co.uk

ISBN   978 184167 462 9

First published in 2011

Copyright © 2011 Ransom Publishing Ltd.

Illustrations copyright © 2011 Jorge Mongiovi and Ulises Carpintero

Printed in India by Imprint Digital Ltd.
Originally published in 1998 by Stanley Thornes Publishers Ltd.

A CIP catalogue record of this book is available from the British Library.

The rights of David Orme to be identified as the author and of Jorge Mongiovi and Ulises Carpintero to be identified as the illustrators of this Work have been asserted by them in accordance with sections 77 and 78 of the Copyright, Design and Patents Act 1988.

CONTENTS

Moving in	5
What they found in the cellar	9
Blood	17
A face with no flesh	23
The dark shape	29
The gallows	33
'Mother, help me!'	39
The burial	43

NOT FOR THE PUBLIC TO KNOW
TOP SECRET
ZONE 13 FILES ONLY

1

MOVING IN

Jodie and Steve were pleased when they heard about the new house their parents had bought. It was big, and had a large garden. It was out in the country, at a place where four roads met.

The family was in the car on the way to the house. Jodie was looking at a map.

'What does 'gallows' mean?' she asked.

'It's the thing they used to hang people on,' said Mum. 'Why do you want to know?'

'Our house is at a place called Gallows Corner.'

'There must have been a gallows there,' said Dad. 'Years ago, they often used to hang people at crossroads.'

'I hope it isn't still there!' said Steve.

'I hope it is!' said Jodie. 'It would be very useful when little brothers start annoying me!'

They started their usual fight. As always, Dad said he would stop the car and throw them out if they didn't stop. They knew he never would.

ooo//ooo

It took two days to move all the furniture in. The whole family was pleased with their new home.

'It's so quiet here, after living in town,' said Mum. 'It will take ages to get used to it.'

Steve's bedroom was at the front of the house. His window looked out over the crossroads. His new room was strange at first. It was hard to get to sleep.

One night, in the first week in the house, Steve was reading in bed. Outside, the wind was blowing. Steve heard a strange noise. He got out of bed and looked out of the window.

There was strange, black shadow hanging by the front gate. It creaked as it swung in the wind.

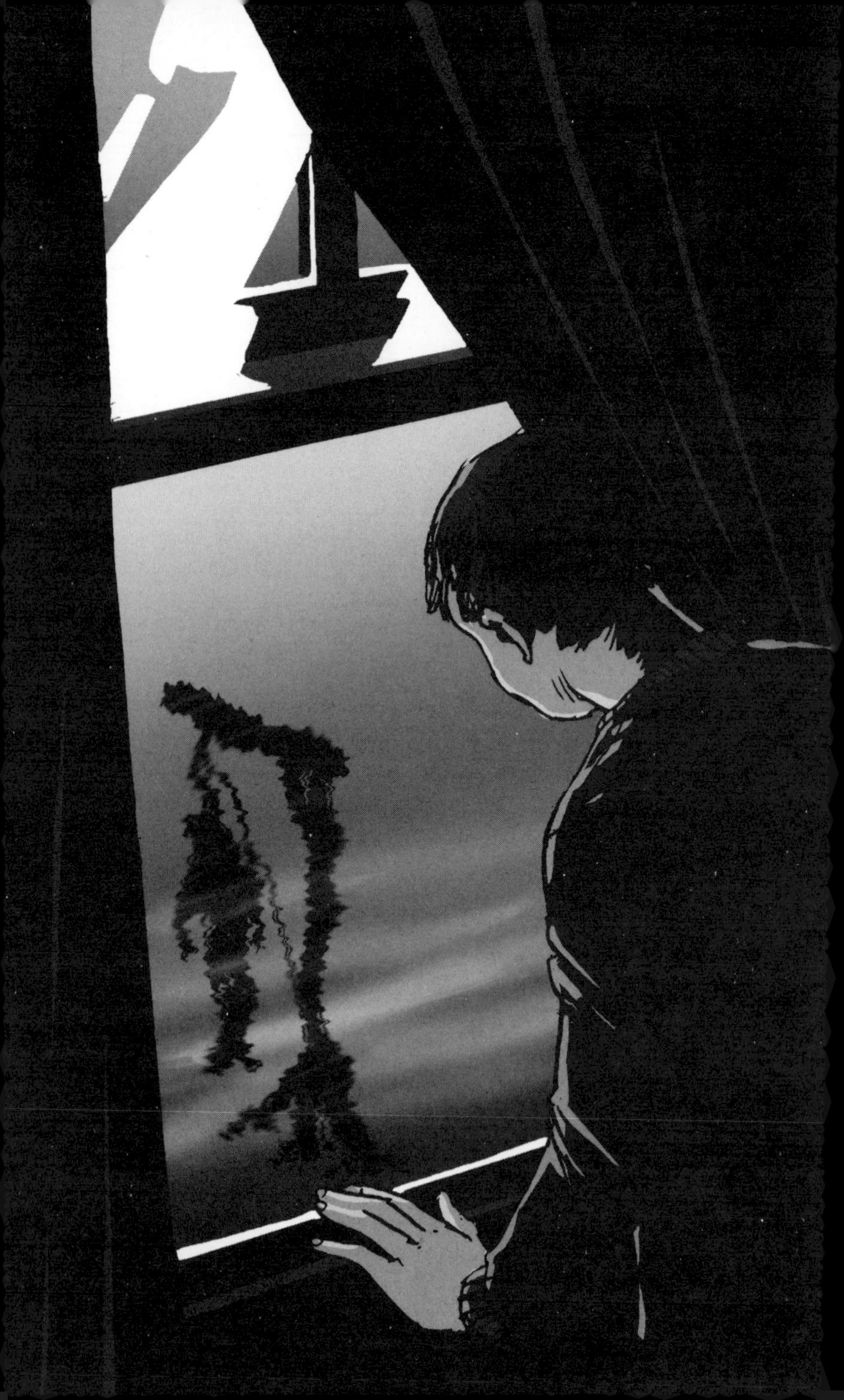

2
WHAT THEY FOUND IN THE CELLAR

It was difficult to see what it was in the dark. It looked like a human figure, but it was in the air, not on the ground. Its feet were swinging about in the wind. Its head was leaning to one side.

Steve blinked. The strange shadow had gone. He remembered what Mum and Dad had said on the journey to the house. A gallows was the thing they hanged people from.

The shadow had looked like someone swinging from a rope.

He looked again. He could see the gate, and the crossroads on the other side of it. But there were no dark shadows.

'It must be my imagination,' he thought. There's nothing there now.

ooo//ooo

When Steve fell asleep, he had a dream about people hanging. They were swinging in the wind. They had tight ropes around their necks. Their faces were swollen. Their tongues were hanging out of their mouths.

Steve didn't say anything the next day. He thought the family would laugh at him.

The house had a big cellar. Mum and Dad had promised Jodie and Steve that they could

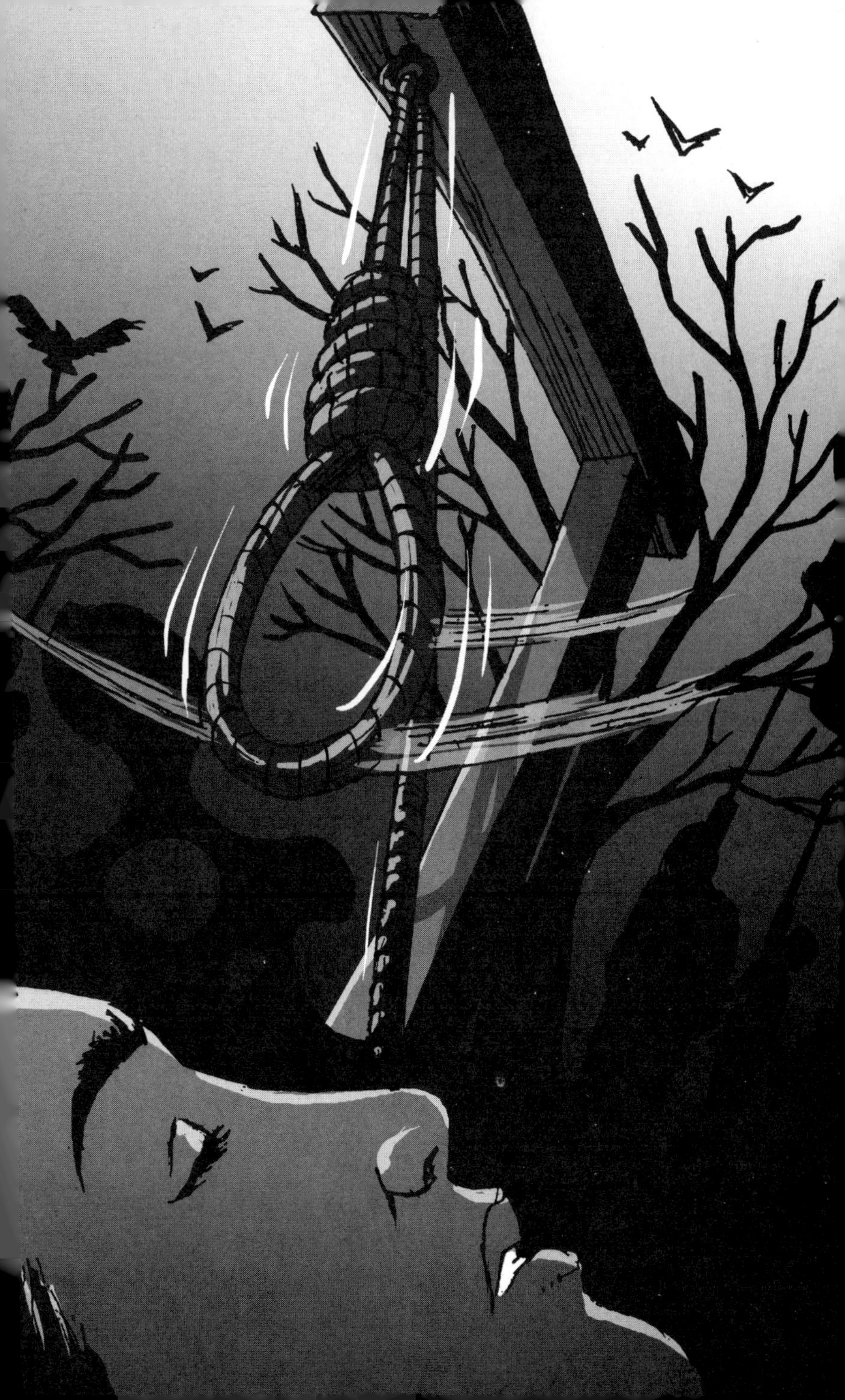

have it as their own space. They decided to start clearing it out.

The cellar was at the front of the house. It was full of boxes and rubbish. An old lady had lived in the house before them and she never threw anything away.

'We'll get Mum and Dad to have a big bonfire in the garden and burn all this lot,' Jodie said.

One wall of the cellar was piled up with rubbish almost to the ceiling. It took a lot of clearing.

'Phew, what a stink!' said Steve.

They had got to the wall at last. It was built of red bricks. They were old and crumbly. A terrible smell came from the wall.

They called Dad down to look at it.

'It can't be the drains that are making the smell,' he said. 'They are at the back of the house.'

One of the bricks was loose. Steve pulled at it. It fell to the floor and broke into pieces. The smell got much worse.

They all yelled in horror.

Hundreds of maggots were crawling out of the hole.

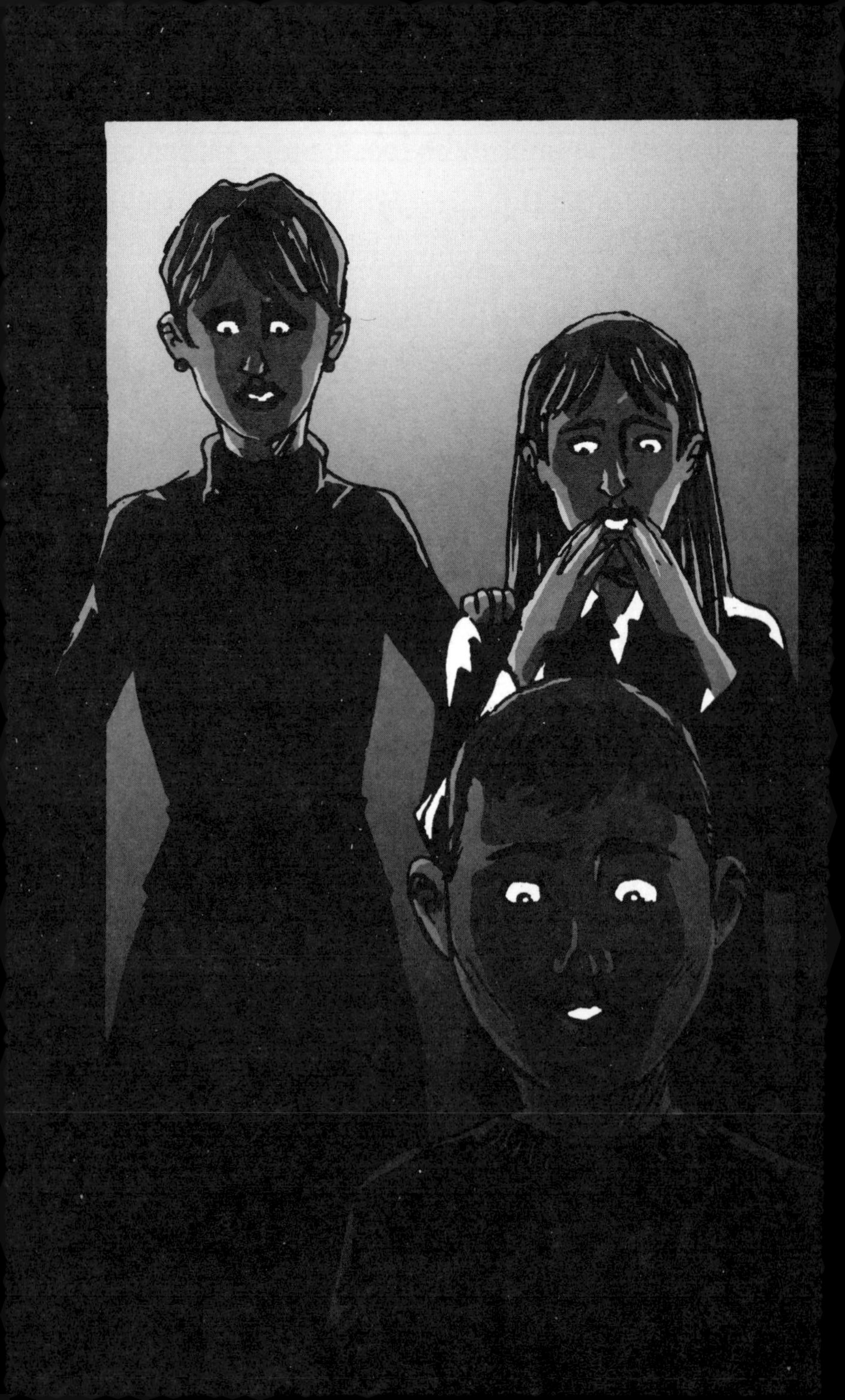

3

BLOOD

Dad went off to buy some cement to mend the wall.

Mum and Jodie were annoyed with Steve and said it was all his fault.

'Trust you to start pulling bricks out,' they said.

Steve sulked at first, but soon cheered up. He was put in charge of the bonfire. He would enjoy that! The smell in the cellar made it too bad to work there.

He was still thinking about what he had seen in the night. It had looked just like a gallows, with a body hanging from it.

Then he remembered something else. The cellar was at the front of the house. That wall was just under the place he had seen the shadow!

ooo//ooo

Dad arrived home with the cement.

They all went down to the cellar again. When they got there, they all had a shock.

There were no more maggots.

This time, something red was dripping down the wall. It was coming through the cracks in the bricks.

It looked like – blood!

It was running down the wall, faster and faster. A pool of it was collecting on the floor.

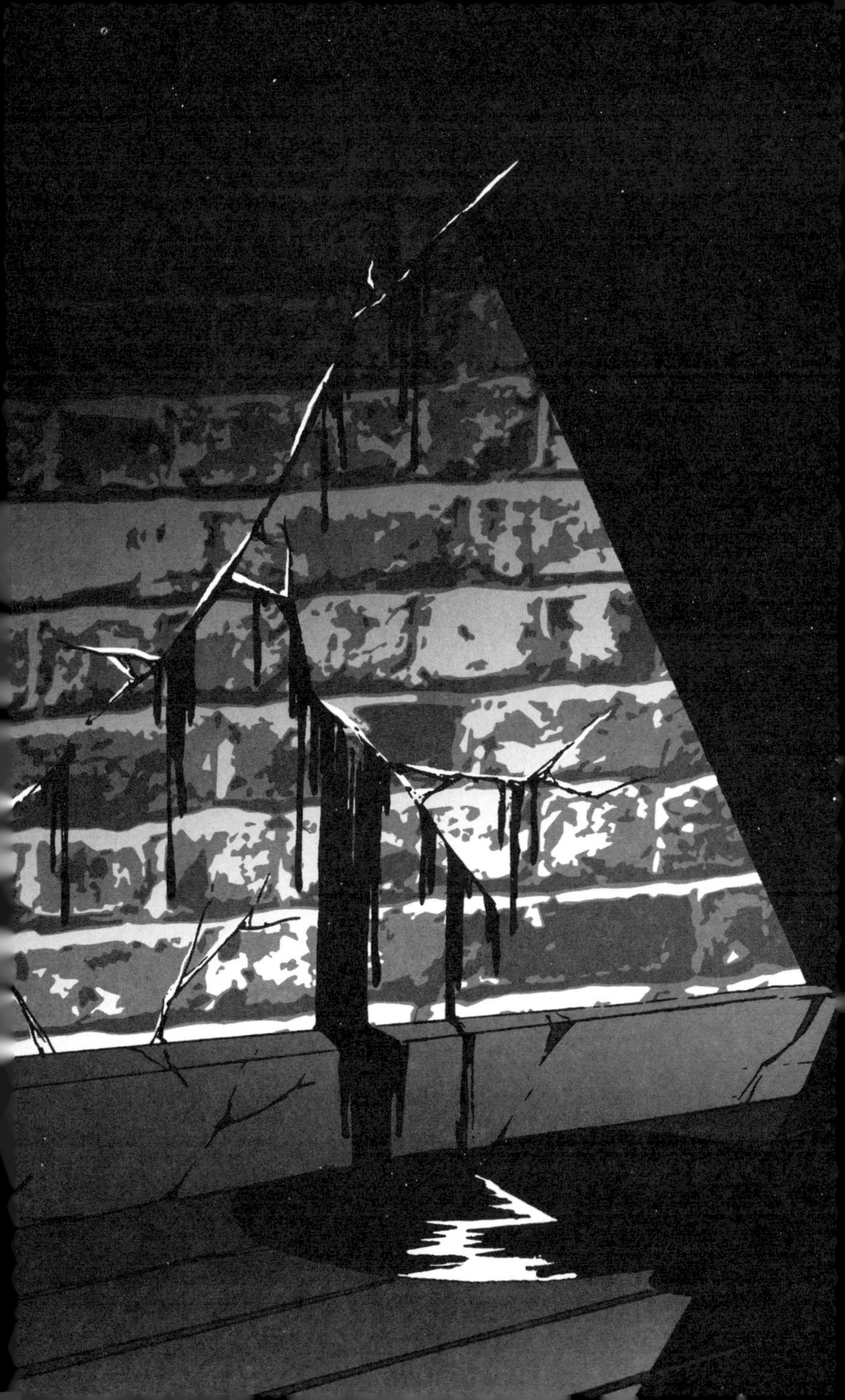

Suddenly Dad yelled out loud.

'Quick! Out of here! The wall's moving!'

The whole wall was crumbling away. Bricks started dropping out of it. The blood poured through more and more.

There was a terrible smell of something rotten.

They all turned and ran up the stairs. There was a door at the top.

The door wouldn't open! Dad kicked at it but it wouldn't move.

Then the light went out.

The cellar had no windows – they were in pitch darkness.

There was a crash below them. Part of the wall must have fallen down. The bad smell got worse.

Jodie was sitting on one of the steps. She tried to make herself very small.

'Please go away!' she whispered. 'Whatever you are, just go away!'

NOT FOR THE PUBLIC TO KNOW
TOP SECRET
ZONE 13 FILES ONLY

4
A FACE WITH NO FLESH

Suddenly, the light came back on.

Dad pushed at the door, and it came open. They all rushed out of the house into the garden.

Everyone was frightened. Dad wasn't feeling at all brave, but he knew that he had to go back down the cellar. A falling wall was serious. The whole house could fall down.

He went carefully down the stairs.

He carried a torch in case the light went out again.

He expected to see blood everywhere. It had poured out of the wall. But there was no sign of it.

There was a big hole in the wall, where lots of the bricks had fallen away.

Behind the wall, Dad could see a dark space in the earth. He flashed his torch into it.

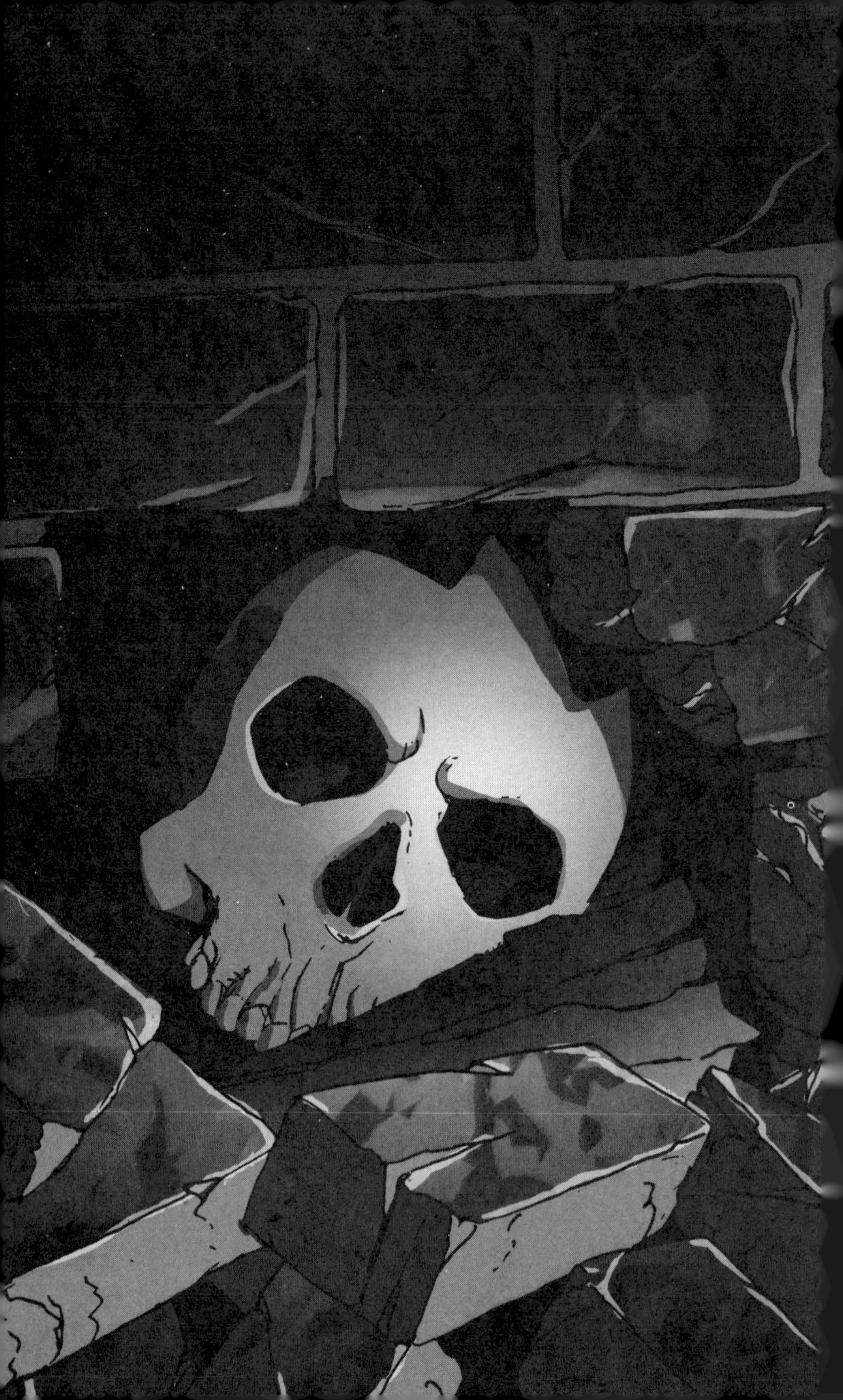

A face looked out at him. A face with no flesh. A skull!

NOT FOR THE PUBLIC TO KNOW
TOP SECRET
ZONE 13 FILES ONLY

5
THE DARK SHAPE

That afternoon, Dad rang round to find a builder to fix the wall. At last he found one. He would start work in the morning.

Steve told Jodie about the shadow in the garden he had seen in the night.

'If you had told me that yesterday, I would have said 'What a load of rubbish',' said Jodie. 'But I'm not sure now.'

ooo//ooo

That night it was windy again. Steve woke up about midnight. He lay in bed for a short time.

Outside, he could hear the creaking sound again. It seemed faint at first, but as he lay there it got louder.

He got up and peeped through the curtains.

He knew what he was going to see.

The dark shape was there again, swinging in the wind.

As he watched, the moon came out. He could see the gallows more clearly now. It had an upright post, and a wooden beam that stuck out. He could see the rope hanging down.

As Steve stood there, a picture came into his head.

He saw faces, looking up at him. They were laughing. At the back of the crowd, a woman was crying. He felt something rough around

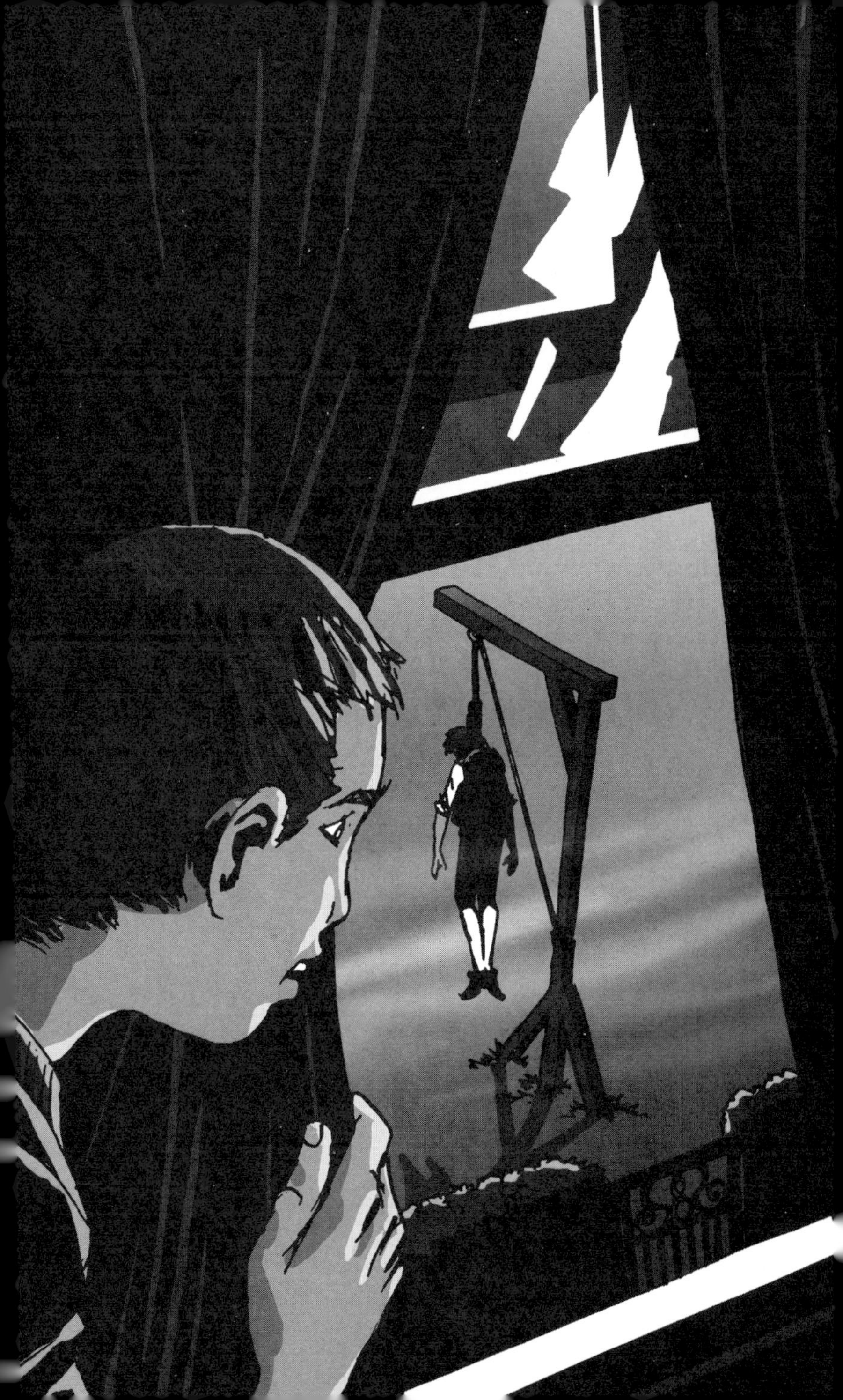

his neck. He was swinging in the air. He couldn't breathe. He was choking, choking ...

Suddenly he was back in his room. He still had a horrible choking feeling. He breathed in great gulps of air.

He rushed to get Jodie. He told her what he had seen.

'Come and see it from my bedroom window,' he said.

'No,' said Jodie. 'Let's get a proper look. I'm going outside!'

6

THE GALLOWS

They didn't want to wake their parents. They crept down and opened the front door. The wind was still blowing. The moon was covered by cloud again. They couldn't see anything at first, but soon their eyes got used to the darkness.

'There it is!' said Steve. 'By the front gate!'

The dark figure was still hanging there. They crept closer. They could see the gallows. It was fixed in the ground just by the gate.

They could see the rope. It was around the neck of the person hanging there.

The neck seemed thin. It was as if someone had taken a paper bag and twisted the top round and round.

It wasn't a full-grown person. It was a small figure – about Steve's size.

Steve stayed back. He felt himself shaking with fear.

He watched as Jodie went nearer. He wanted to call her back, but he couldn't speak. Jodie walked closer and closer.

The figure swung round, and Jodie saw its face.

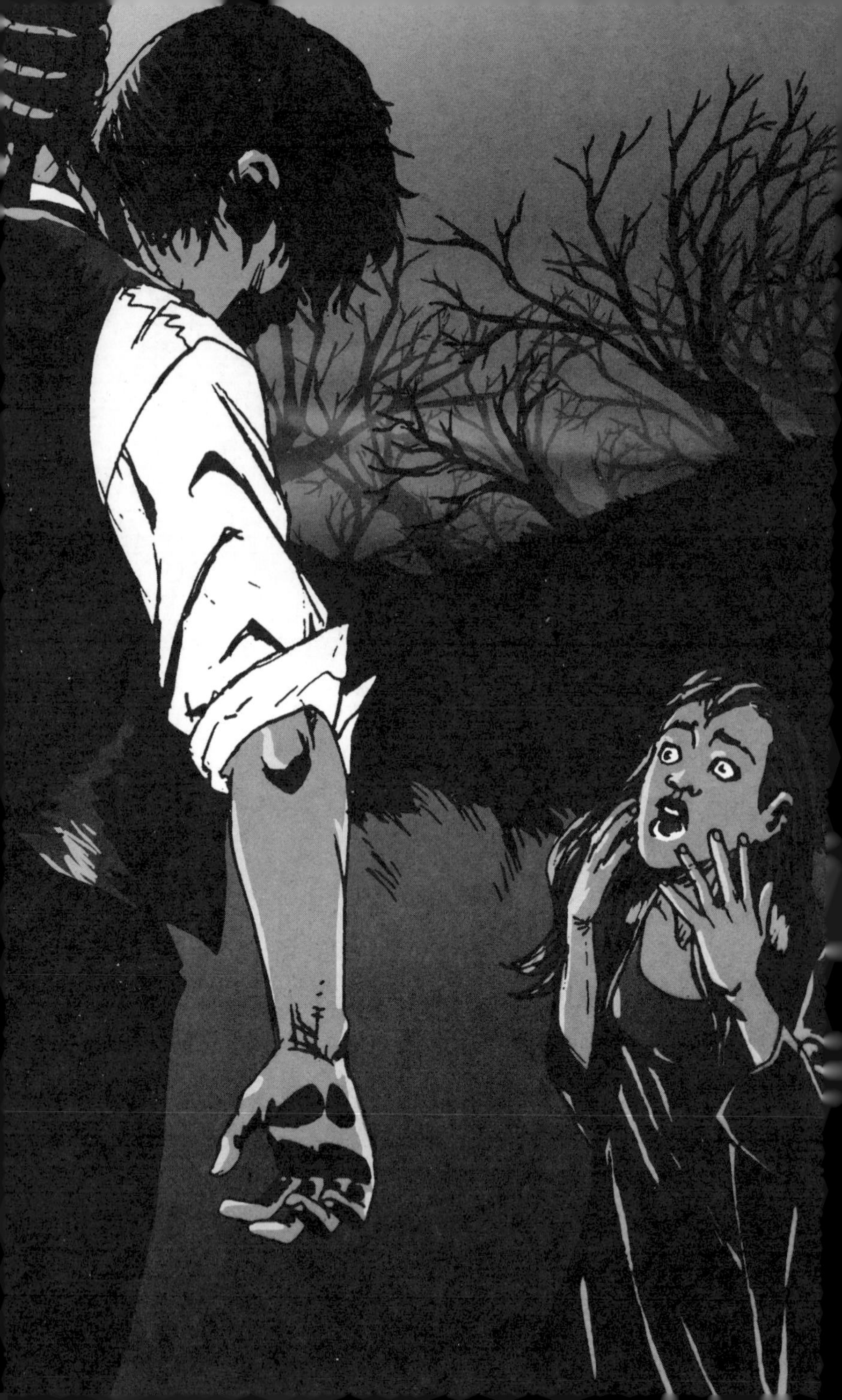

A black tongue hung out of its mouth. The face was swollen and horrible.

But Jodie knew the face.

It was Steve's.

NOT FOR THE PUBLIC TO KNOW
TOP SECRET
ZONE 13 FILES ONLY

7
'MOTHER, HELP ME!'

Jodie must have fainted at that moment, but Steve said later that she didn't fall. She just stood there, staring.

For Jodie, it was no longer the middle of the night. It was early morning.

A crowd of people were marching up the lane. A boy was being pushed along. His hands were tied together. Everyone was wearing rough clothes.

A man in a black gown was reading from a book.

Jodie looked at the boy. She realised that it wasn't Steve after all. He looked very much like him though. The boy was the same height, and had the same colour hair.

She looked at the boy's face. He looked terrified. Her brother had looked like that when they saw the blood in the cellar.

Some people were laughing. It looked as if they were having a fun day out.

The crowd reached the gallows. They forced the boy to stand on a stool. A big, rough man put a rope round his neck. The man in black was whispering in his ear.

At last the boy spoke. He had a strange accent, but Jodie understood what he said.

'It wasn't me! You've got the wrong boy! I'm innocent!'

The boy looked towards the back of the crowd. A woman stood there, weeping.

'Mother! Help me!'

The rough man kicked away the stool. A cheer came from the crowd.

The wind blew. The boy hung there, swaying backwards and forwards.

8

THE BURIAL

A week later, the family was standing in the churchyard in the nearby village. A vicar was saying prayers over a small coffin. It was lowered into a hole in the ground and covered over.

Jodie had said nothing. She didn't tell anyone what she had seen that night, not even Steve.

ooo//ooo

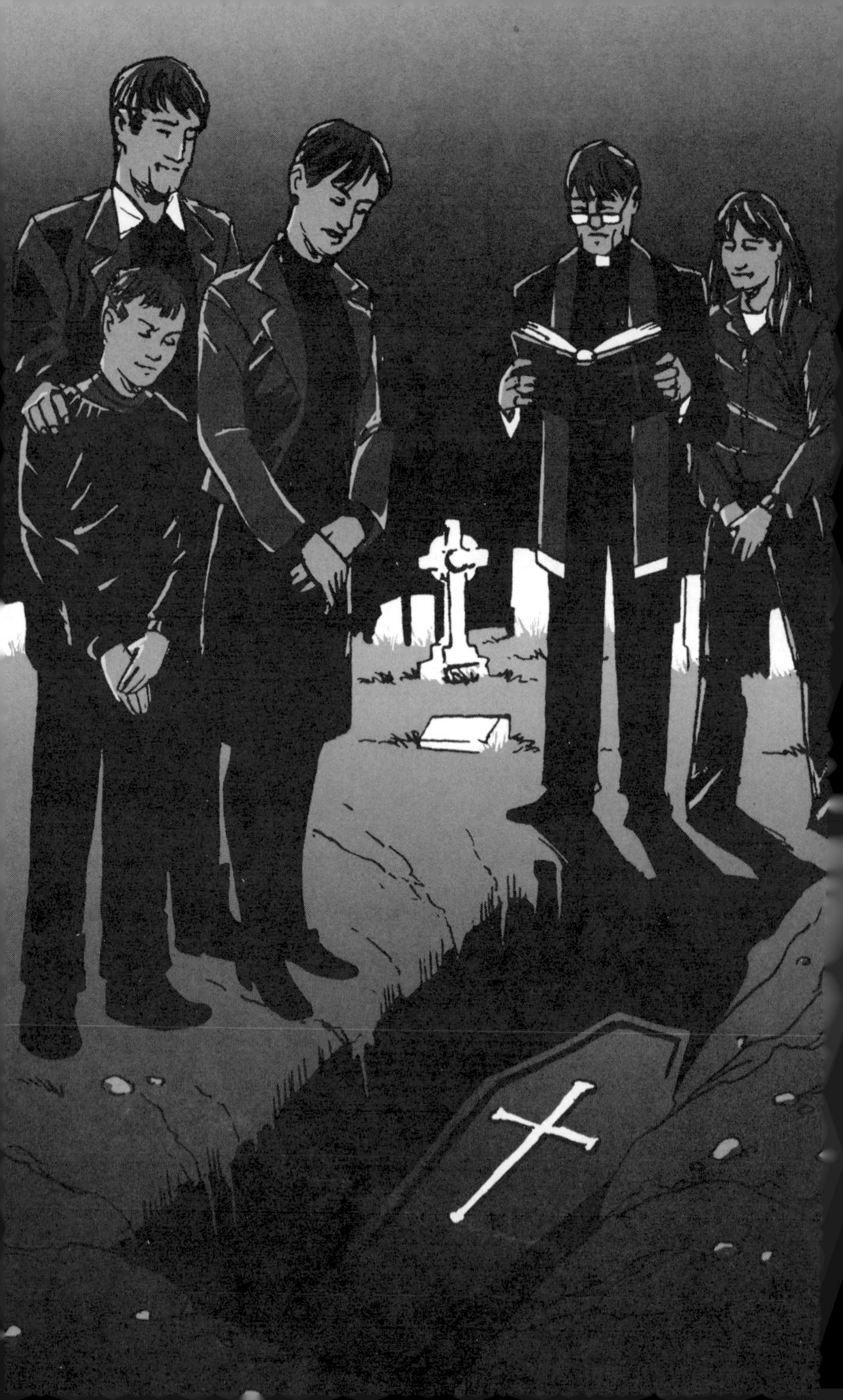

It had been another boy called Stephen. Three hundred years ago, he had been hanged for stealing a sheep.

His body had been thrown into a pit next to the gallows. People thought that criminals didn't deserve a proper burial.

Jodie knew that he hadn't stolen the sheep. She also knew that he wanted to be buried in the graveyard in the village, where all his family had been buried.

Jodie's parents thought that the bones they had found should be buried properly. They had contacted the vicar and he had agreed with them.

'We don't know the name, so we can't put a stone over the grave,' the vicar had said.

But Jodie knew.

She whispered her own little prayer over the grave.

'Stephen,' she said. 'You can rest in peace now.'

NOT FOR THE PUBLIC TO KNOW
TOP SECRET
ZONE 13 FILES ONLY

ABOUT THE AUTHOR

David Orme is an expert on strange, unexplained events. For his protection (and yours) we cannot show a photograph of him.

David created the Zone 13 files to record the cases he studied. Some of these files really do involve aliens, but many do not. Aliens are not everywhere. Just in most places.

These stories are all taken from the Zone 13 files. They will not be here for long. Read them while you can.

But don't close your eyes when you go to sleep at night. **They** will be watching you.